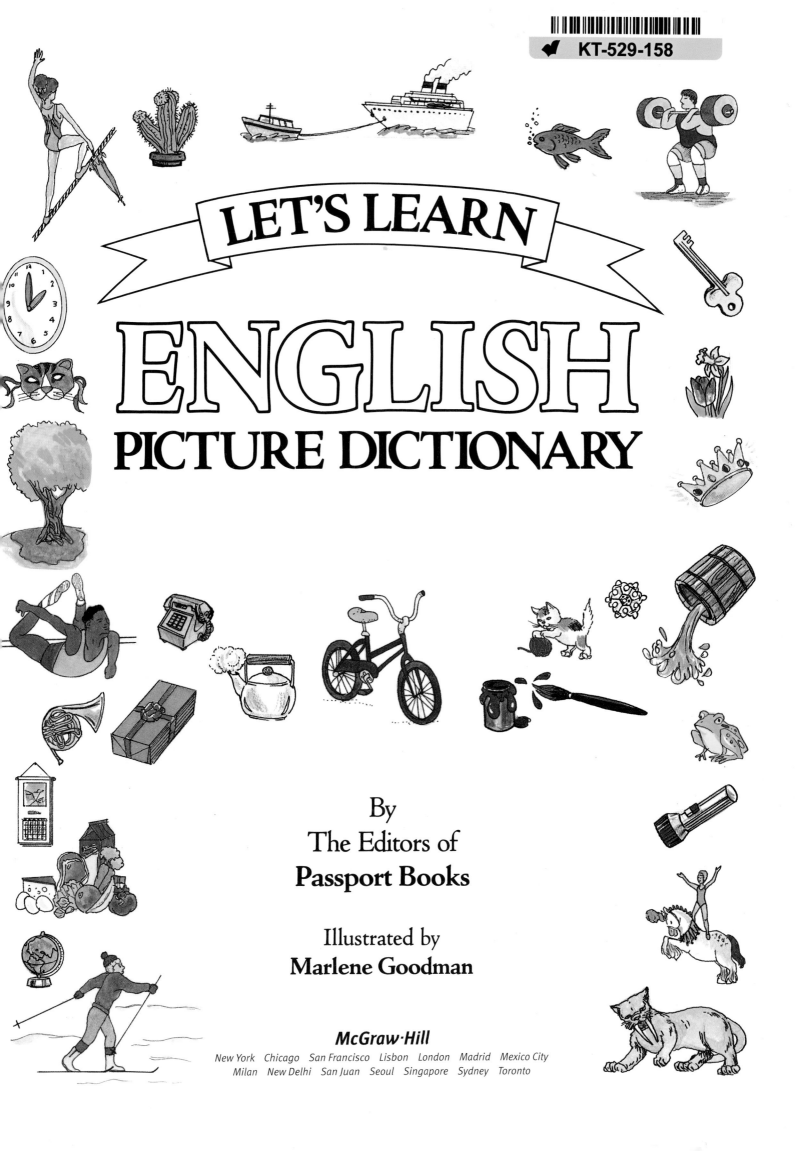

LET'S LEARN
ENGLISH
PICTURE DICTIONARY

By
The Editors of
Passport Books

Illustrated by
Marlene Goodman

McGraw·Hill

New York   Chicago   San Francisco   Lisbon   London   Madrid   Mexico City
Milan   New Delhi   San Juan   Seoul   Singapore   Sydney   Toronto

Welcome to the *Let's Learn English* Picture Dictionary!

Here's an exciting way for you to learn more than 1,500 words that will help you speak about many of your favorite subjects. With these words, you will be able to talk about your house, sports, outer space, the ocean, and many more subjects.

This dictionary is fun to use. On each page, you will see drawings with the words that describe them underneath. These drawings are usually part of a large, colorful scene. See if you can find all the words in the big scene! You will enjoy looking at the pictures more and more as you learn new words.

At the back of the book, you will find an Index, an alphabetical list of all the words in the dictionary. You can look up words in the Index and find out on which page each word is located.

This is a book you can look at over and over again, and each time you look, you will find something new. You'll be able to talk about people, places, and things you know, and you'll learn lots of new words as you go along!

The McGraw·Hill Companies

Library of Congress Cataloging-in-Publication Data

Let's learn English picture dictionary / by the editors of Passport
    Books ; illustrated by Marlene Goodman.
            p.   cm.
        Includes index.
        ISBN 0-07-140822-3
        1. Picture dictionaries, English—Juvenile literature.
    I. Title: English picture dictionary.   II. Goodman, Marlene.
    III. Passport Books.

    PE1629.L47   2004
    423'.17—dc22   2004052637

Illustrations by Terrie Meider
7. Clothing; 15. People in Our Community; 18. Sports; 28. Colors;
29. The Family Tree; 30. Shapes; 31. Numbers; 32. Map of the World

16 17 18 WKT/WKT 18 17

ISBN 0-07-140822-3

McGraw-Hill books are available at special quantity discounts to use as
premiums and sales promotions, or for use in corporate training
programs. For more information, please write to the Director of Special
Sales, Professional Publishing, McGraw-Hill, Two Penn Plaza, New York,
NY 10121-2298. Or contact your local bookstore.

This book is printed on acid-free paper.

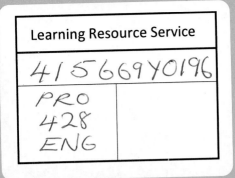

Table of Contents

1. Our Classroom

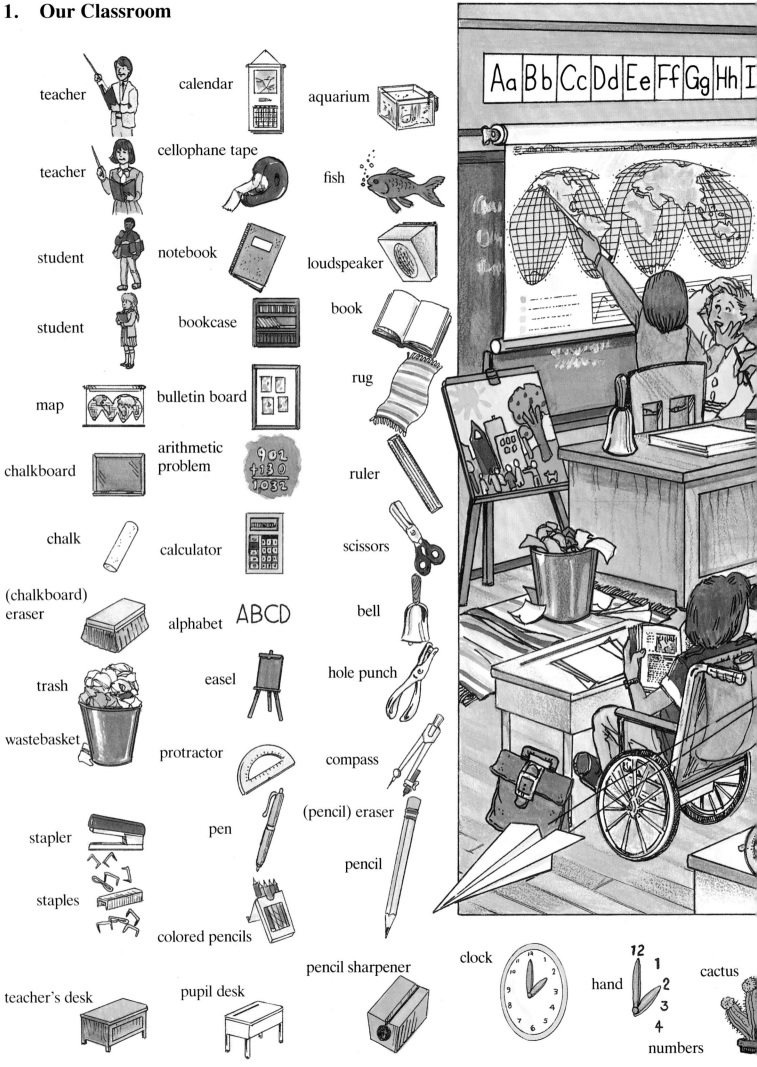

teacher

teacher

student

student

map

chalkboard

chalk

(chalkboard) eraser

trash

wastebasket

stapler

staples

teacher's desk

calendar

cellophane tape

notebook

bookcase

bulletin board

arithmetic problem

calculator

alphabet ABCD

easel

protractor

pen

colored pencils

pupil desk

aquarium

fish

loudspeaker

book

rug

ruler

scissors

bell

hole punch

compass

(pencil) eraser

pencil

pencil sharpener

clock

hand

cactus

numbers

plant

glue

globe

picture

paint   paintbrush

paper

crayon

2. Our House

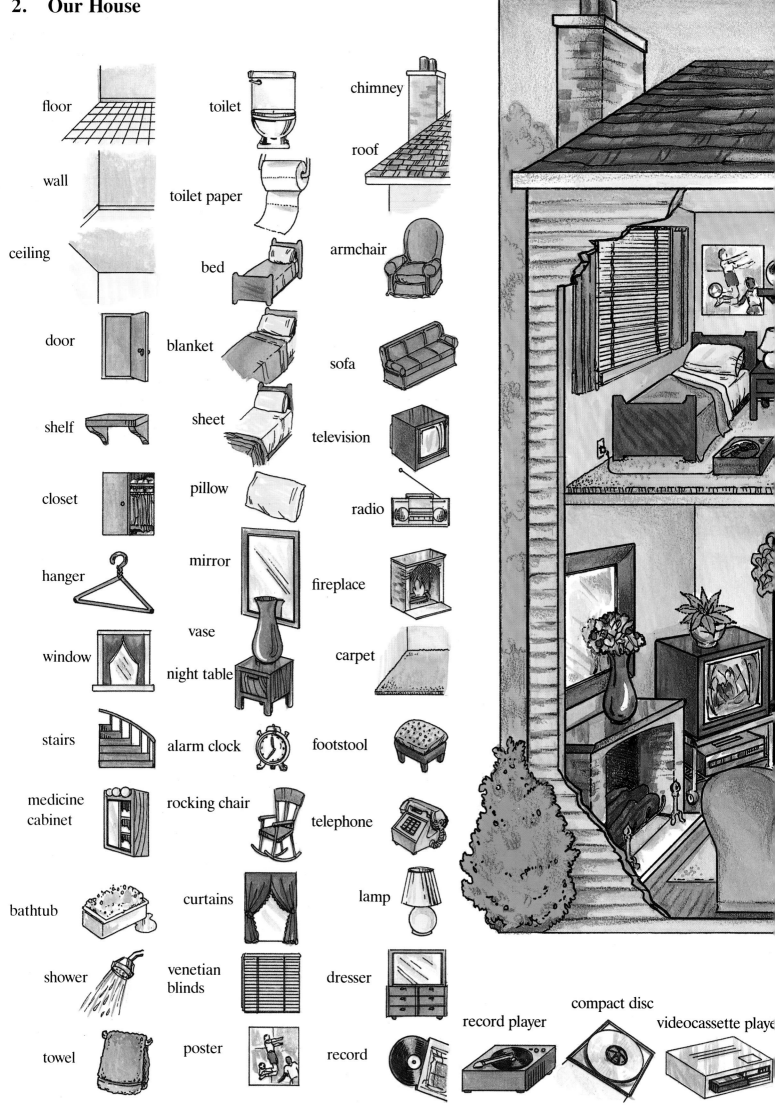

floor

wall

ceiling

door

shelf

closet

hanger

window

stairs

medicine cabinet

bathtub

shower

towel

toilet

toilet paper

bed

blanket

sheet

pillow

mirror

vase

night table

alarm clock

rocking chair

curtains

venetian blinds

poster

chimney

roof

armchair

sofa

television

radio

fireplace

carpet

footstool

telephone

lamp

dresser

record player

compact disc

videocassette player

record

bedroom **bathroom** **living room** **dining room** **kitchen**

sette tape cassette player

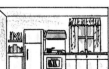

3. The Kitchen

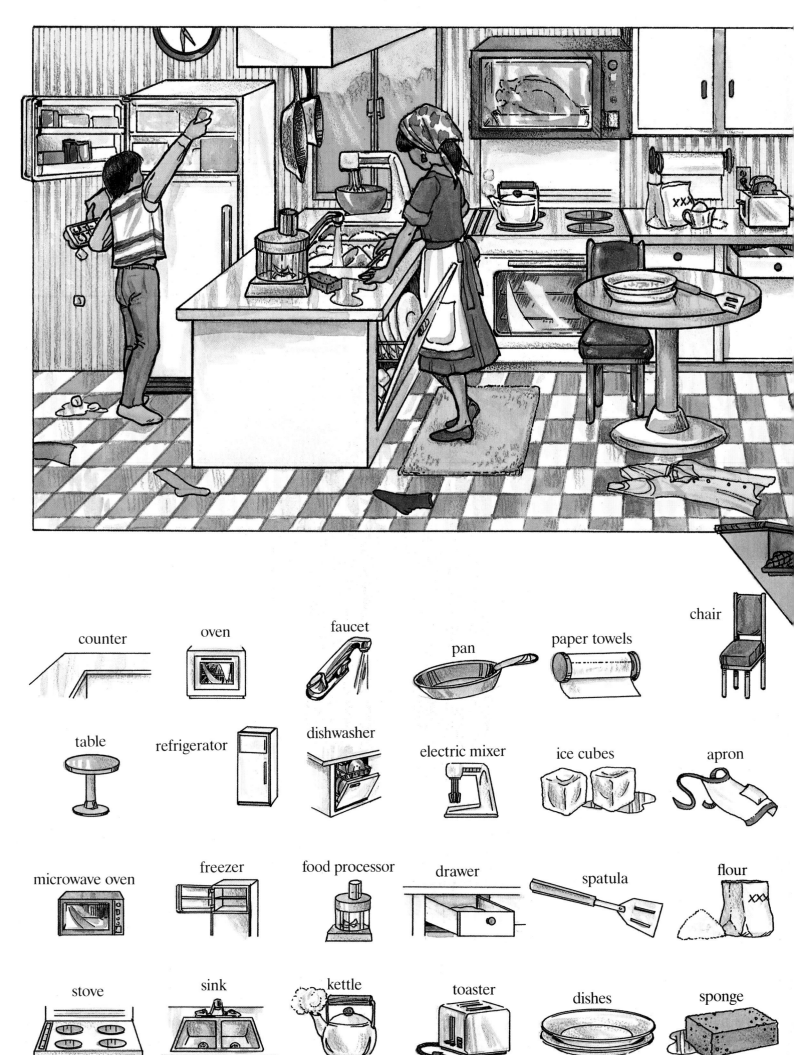

counter

oven

faucet

pan

paper towels

chair

table

refrigerator

dishwasher

electric mixer

ice cubes

apron

microwave oven

freezer

food processor

drawer

spatula

flour

stove

sink

kettle

toaster

dishes

sponge

washing machine

iron

screw

toolbox

laundry detergent

laundry

broom

mop

screwdriver

wrench

wood

board

dustpan

electrical outlet

cuum cleaner

drill

sandpaper

flashlight

hammer

brick

ironing board

clothes dryer

nail

file

tape measure

saw

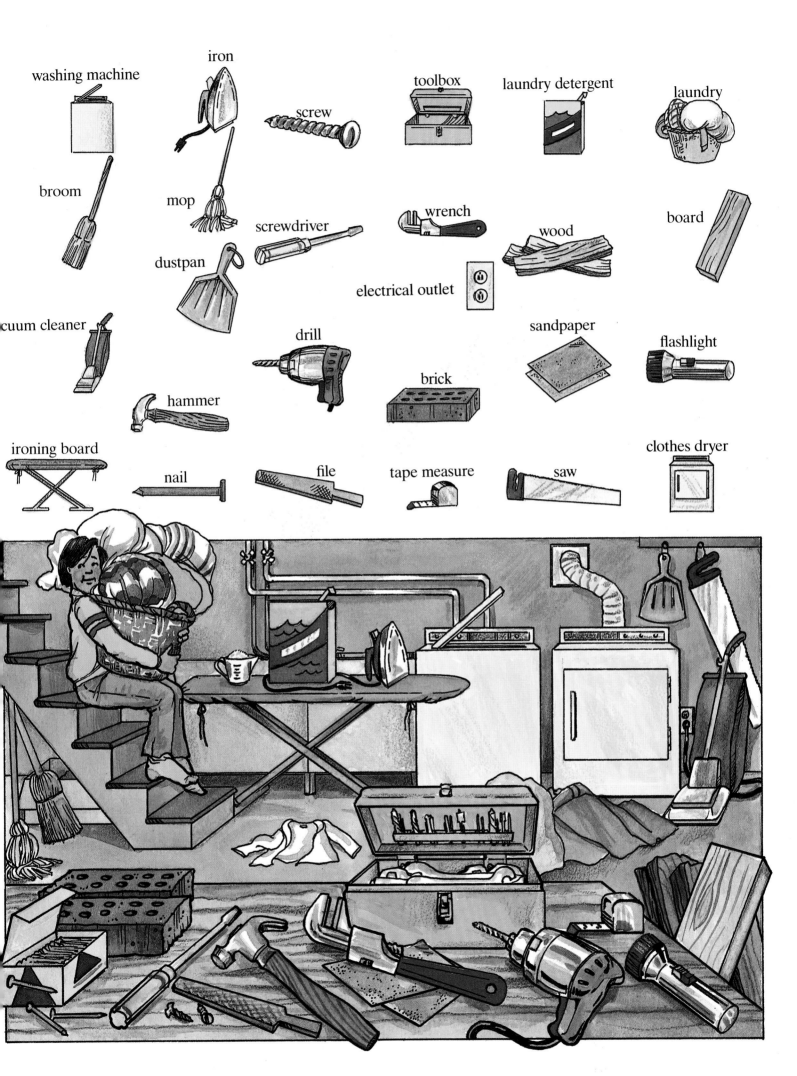

4. The Attic

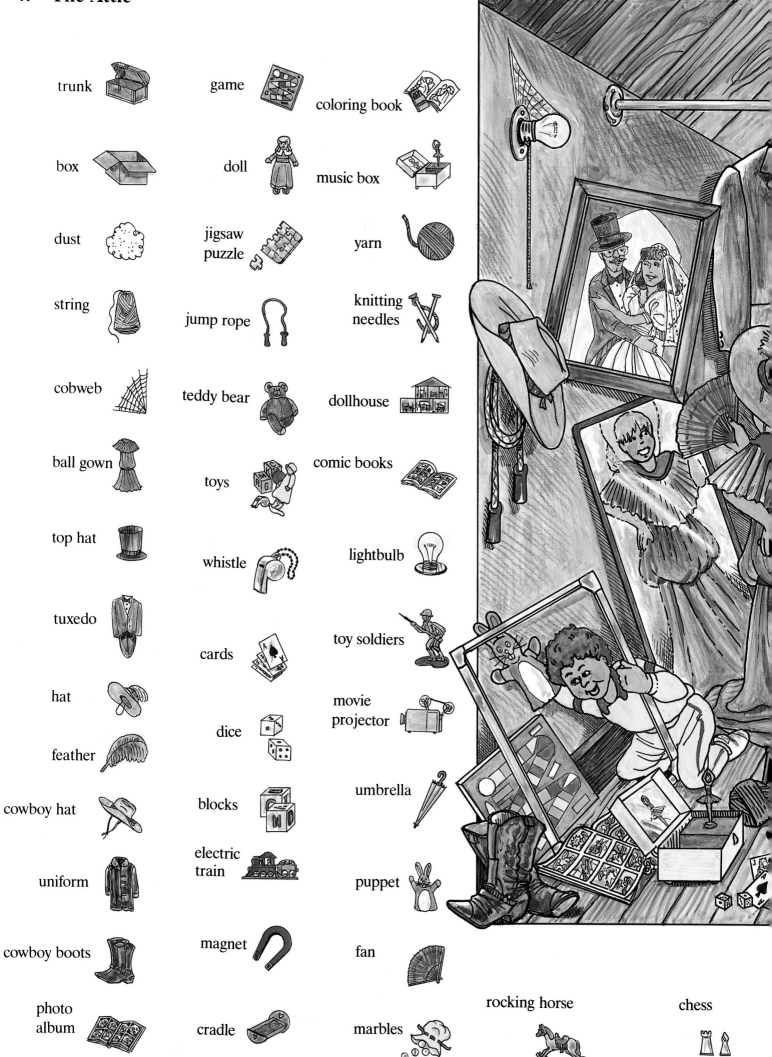

trunk

game

coloring book

box

doll

music box

dust

jigsaw puzzle

yarn

string

jump rope

knitting needles

cobweb

teddy bear

dollhouse

ball gown

toys

comic books

top hat

whistle

lightbulb

tuxedo

cards

toy soldiers

hat

movie projector

dice

feather

umbrella

cowboy hat

blocks

electric train

uniform

puppet

cowboy boots

magnet

fan

photo album

cradle

marbles

rocking horse

chess

photograph

spinning wheel

picture frame

rocking chair

checkers

5. The Four Seasons (Weather)

Winter

snow

sled

ice

snowplow

snowflake

snowmobile

icicle

snowman

shovel

snowball

snowstorm

log

Spring

rain

flowers

rainbow

flowerbed

stem

petal

bird

vegetable garden

worm

raindrop

lightning

Summer

butterfly

fly

fly swatter

fan

sprinkler

grasshopper

lawn mower

barbecue

hammock

yard

deck

garden hose

matches

Fall

wind

leaf

branch

fog

rake

clouds

kite

puddle

mud

bird's nest

bush

6. At the Supermarket

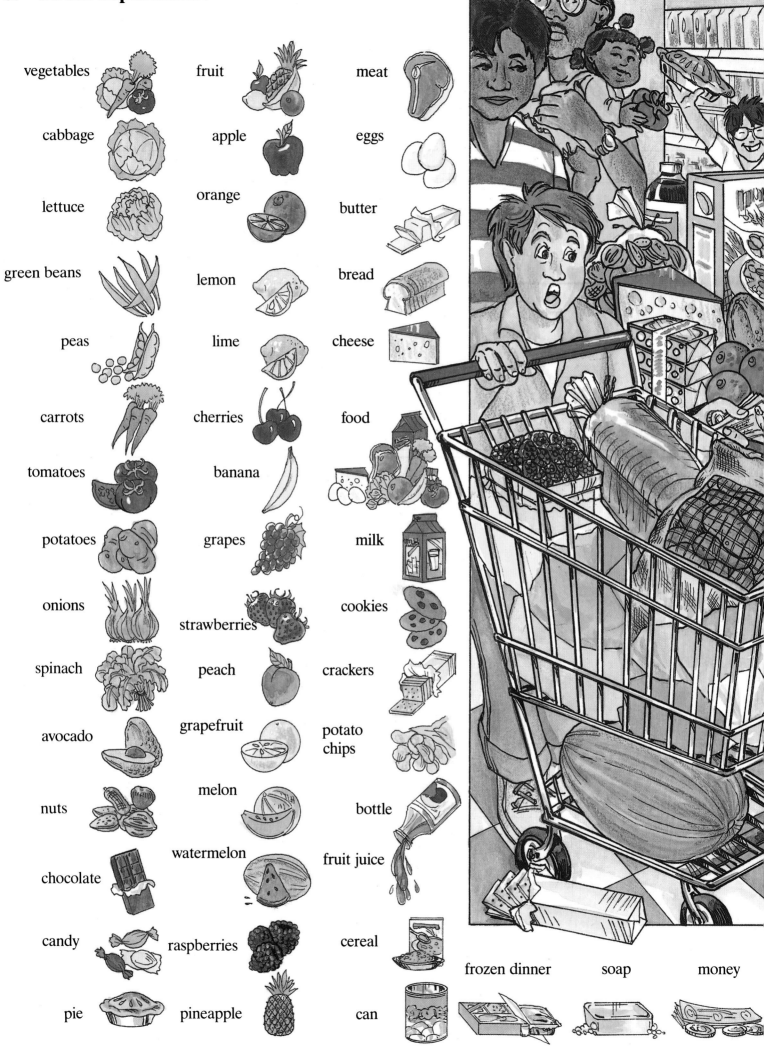

vegetables

cabbage

lettuce

green beans

peas

carrots

tomatoes

potatoes

onions

spinach

avocado

nuts

chocolate

candy

pie

fruit

apple

orange

lemon

lime

cherries

banana

grapes

strawberries

peach

grapefruit

melon

watermelon

raspberries

pineapple

meat

eggs

butter

bread

cheese

food

milk

cookies

crackers

potato chips

bottle

fruit juice

cereal

can

frozen dinner

soap

money

shopping cart

shopping
bag

sign

scale

price

cash
register

cashier

7. Clothing

glasses

buckle belt

pants

underwear

collar

blouse

ring

bracelet

skirt

socks

shoes

necklace

tie

sleeve

dress

bathing suit

shirt

suit

button

earmuffs

gloves

handkerchief

coat

sweater

shoelace

gym shoes

tights

hat

sunglasses

earring

sweatshirt

hood

raincoat

shorts

pocket

zipper

sweatpants

sandals

backpack

T-shirt

umbrella

boots

watch

down vest

scarf

bathrobe

pajamas

jeans

jacket

mittens

hiking boots

cap

8. In the City

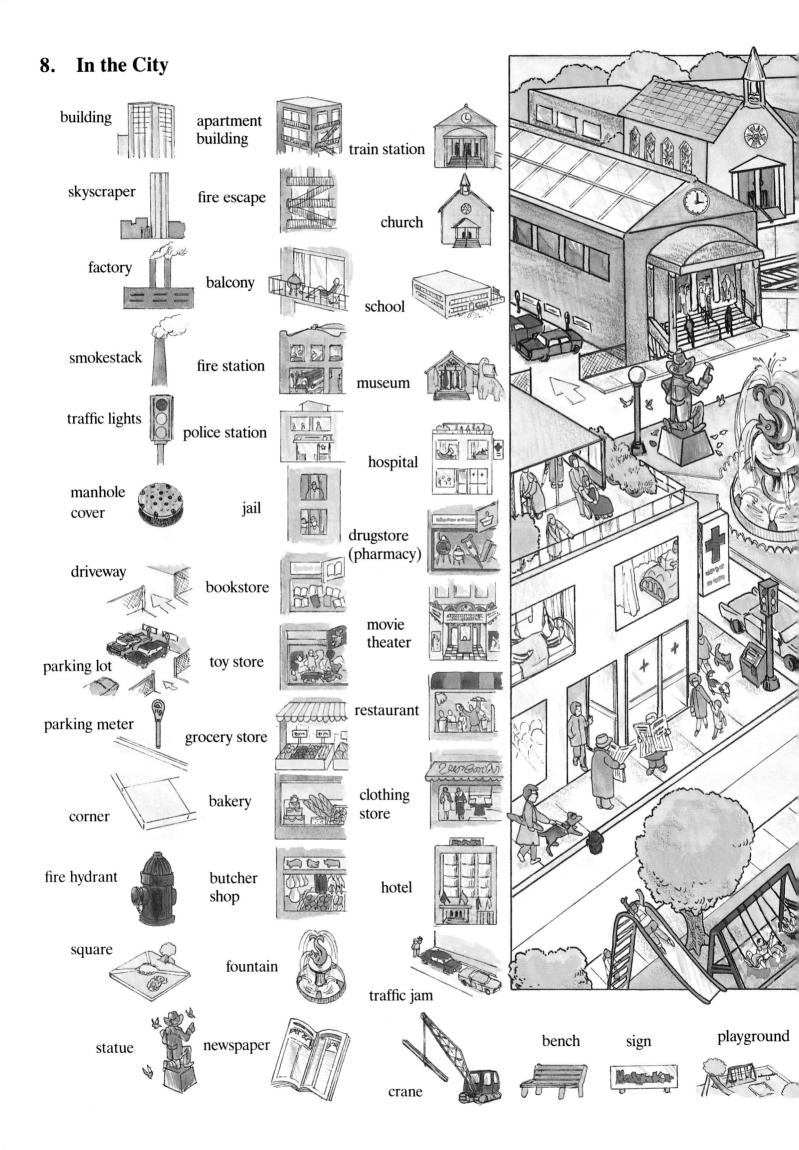

building

apartment building

skyscraper

fire escape

factory

balcony

smokestack

fire station

traffic lights

police station

manhole cover

jail

driveway

bookstore

parking lot

toy store

parking meter

grocery store

corner

bakery

fire hydrant

butcher shop

square

fountain

statue

newspaper

crane

train station

church

school

museum

hospital

drugstore (pharmacy)

movie theater

restaurant

clothing store

hotel

traffic jam

bench

sign

playground

park	jungle gym	swings	seesaw	slide	sandbox	beach

9. In the Country

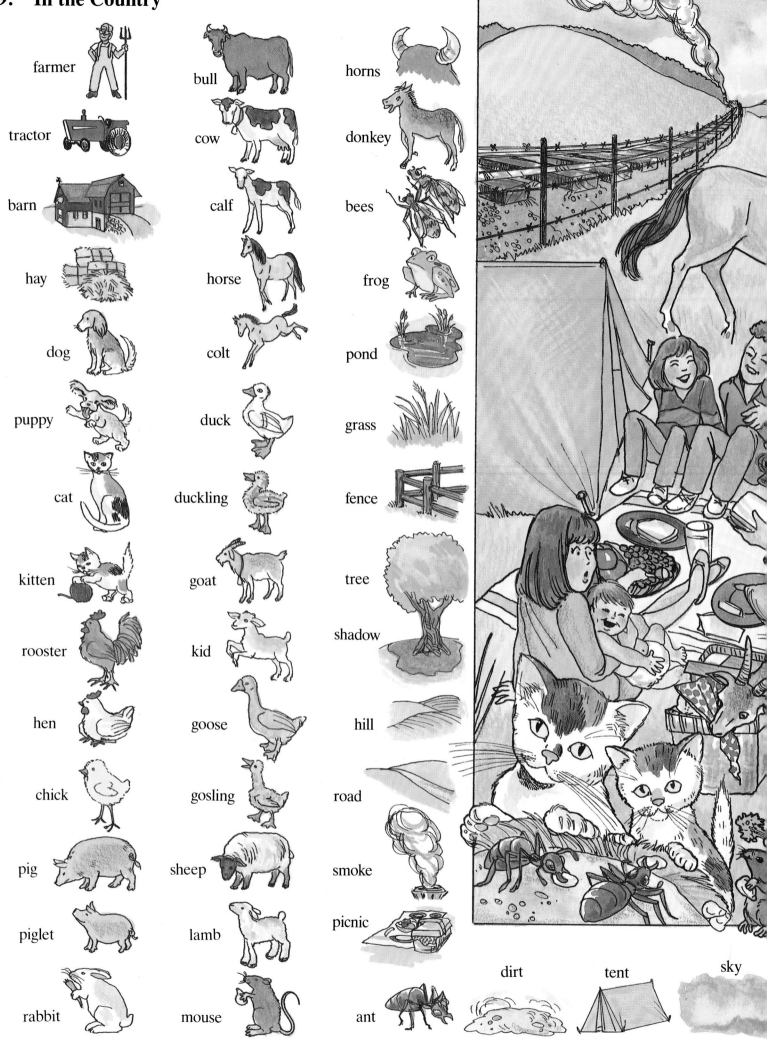

farmer

tractor

barn

hay

dog

puppy

cat

kitten

rooster

hen

chick

pig

piglet

rabbit

bull

cow

calf

horse

colt

duck

duckling

goat

kid

goose

gosling

sheep

lamb

mouse

horns

donkey

bees

frog

pond

grass

fence

tree

shadow

hill

road

smoke

picnic

ant

dirt

tent

sky

train tracks

sleeping bag

man woman

boy

girl

baby

farm

10. In a Restaurant

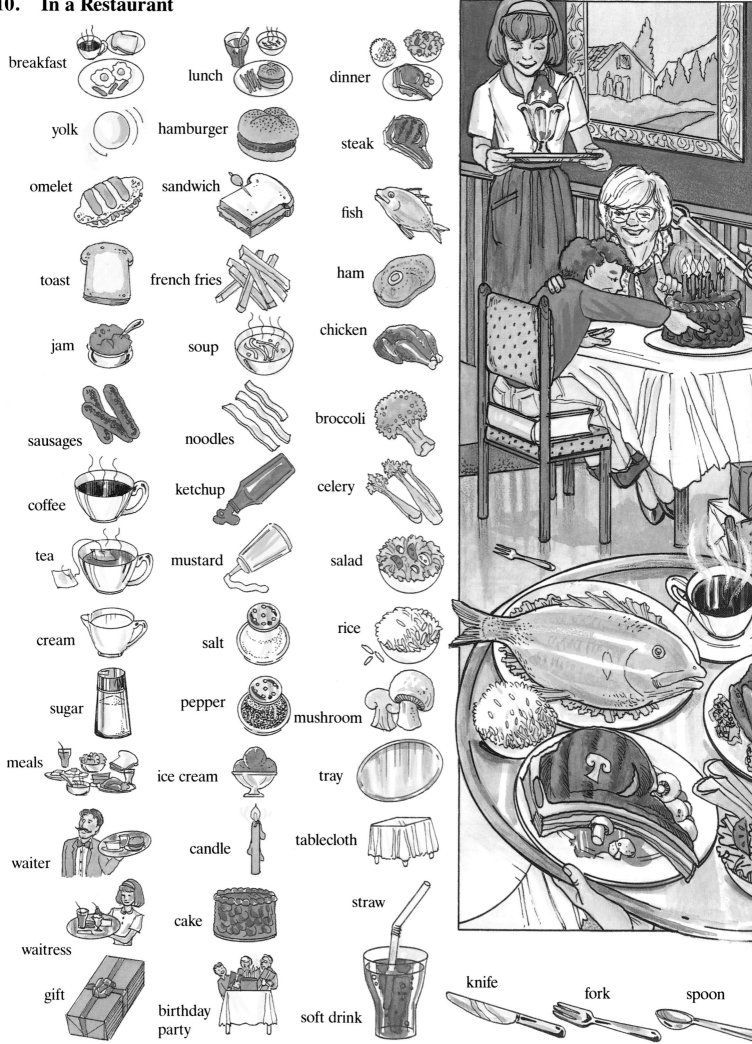

breakfast

lunch

dinner

yolk

hamburger

steak

omelet

sandwich

fish

toast

french fries

ham

jam

soup

chicken

sausages

noodles

broccoli

coffee

ketchup

celery

tea

mustard

salad

cream

salt

rice

sugar

pepper

mushroom

meals

ice cream

tray

waiter

candle

tablecloth

waitress

cake

straw

gift

birthday party

soft drink

knife

fork

spoon

plate

saucer

cup

glass

bowl

napkin

menu

11. The Doctor's Office

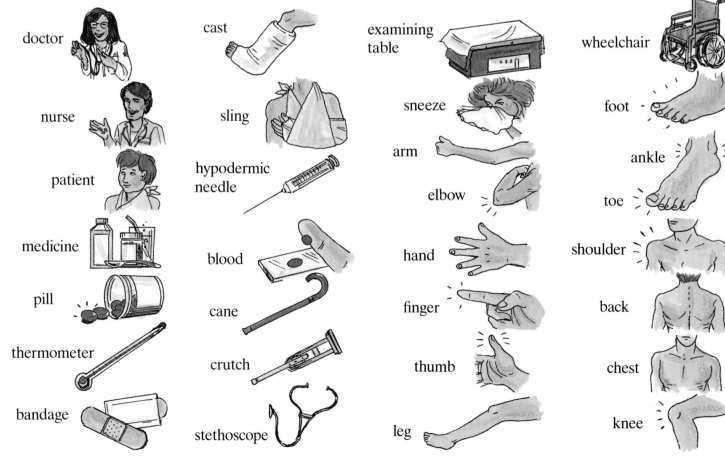

doctor

nurse

patient

medicine

pill

thermometer

bandage

cast

sling

hypodermic needle

blood

cane

crutch

stethoscope

examining table

sneeze

arm

elbow

hand

finger

thumb

leg

wheelchair

foot

ankle

toe

shoulder

back

chest

knee

The Dentist's Office

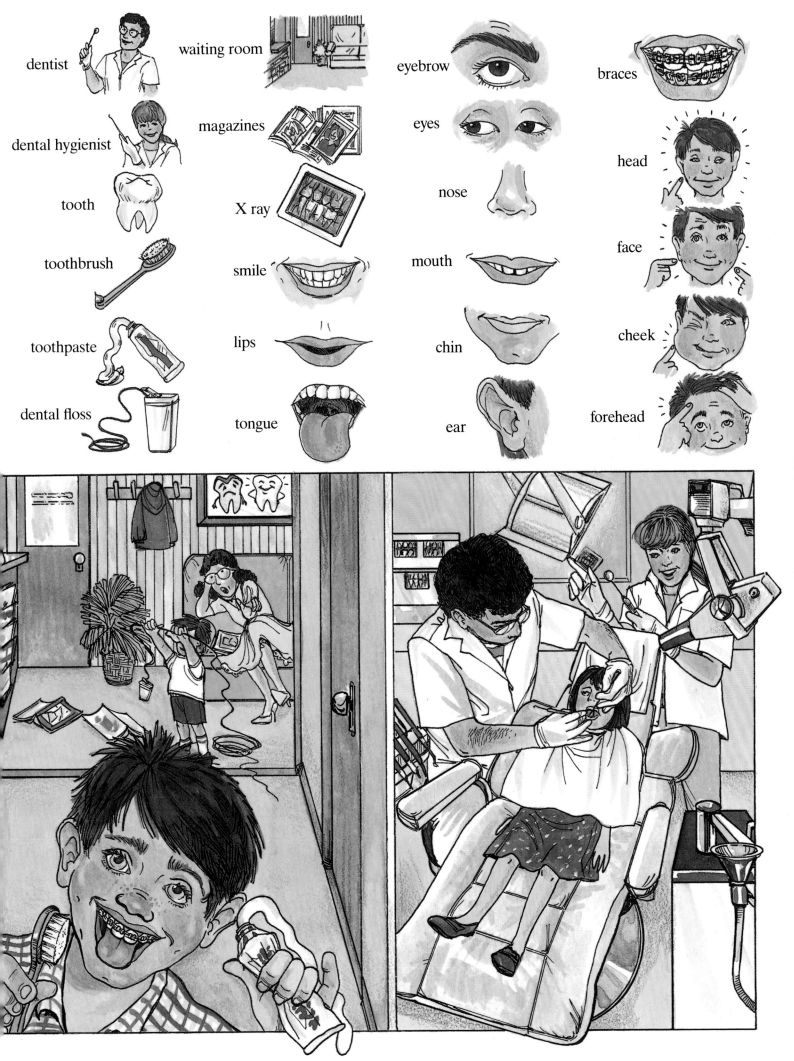

dentist

dental hygienist

tooth

toothbrush

toothpaste

dental floss

waiting room

magazines

X ray

smile

lips

tongue

eyebrow

eyes

nose

mouth

chin

ear

braces

head

face

cheek

forehead

12.   The Barber Shop/Beauty Salon

hairstylist

shampoo

suds

comb

brush

scissors

curlers

curling iron

barber

shaving cream

razor

beard

mousse

manicurist

fingernail

nail polish

lipstick

mascara

powder

hair dryer

bald

mustache

freckles

pedicurist

barrette

braid

wavy

straight

curly

short

long

black

brown

blond

red

toenail

nail clippers

nail file

crew cut

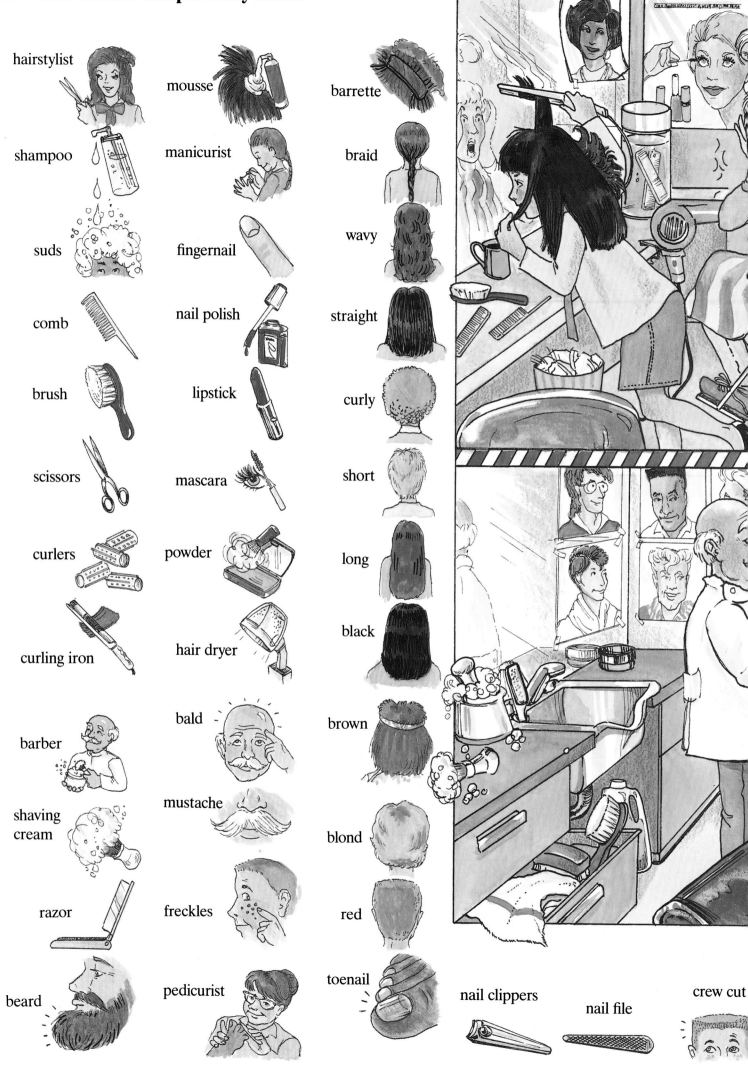

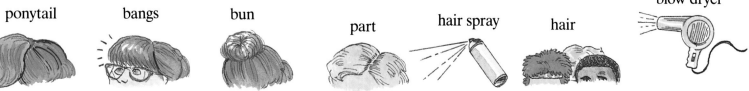

ponytail
bangs
bun
part
hair spray
hair
blow dryer

13. The Post Office

packing tape

package

scale

ink pad

post-office box

rubber stamp

label

rubber band

letter

postcard

string

knot

bow

postmark

phone booth

return address

address

mailbox

zip code

60016

mail slot

mailbag

postal worker

stamp

The Bank

paper clip

security guard

security camera

safe

credit card

typewriter

safety deposit box

notepad

teller

wallet

key

lock

file cabinet

receptionist

bill

coin

check

checkbook

piggy bank

signature

drive-in

automatic teller

14. At the Gas Station

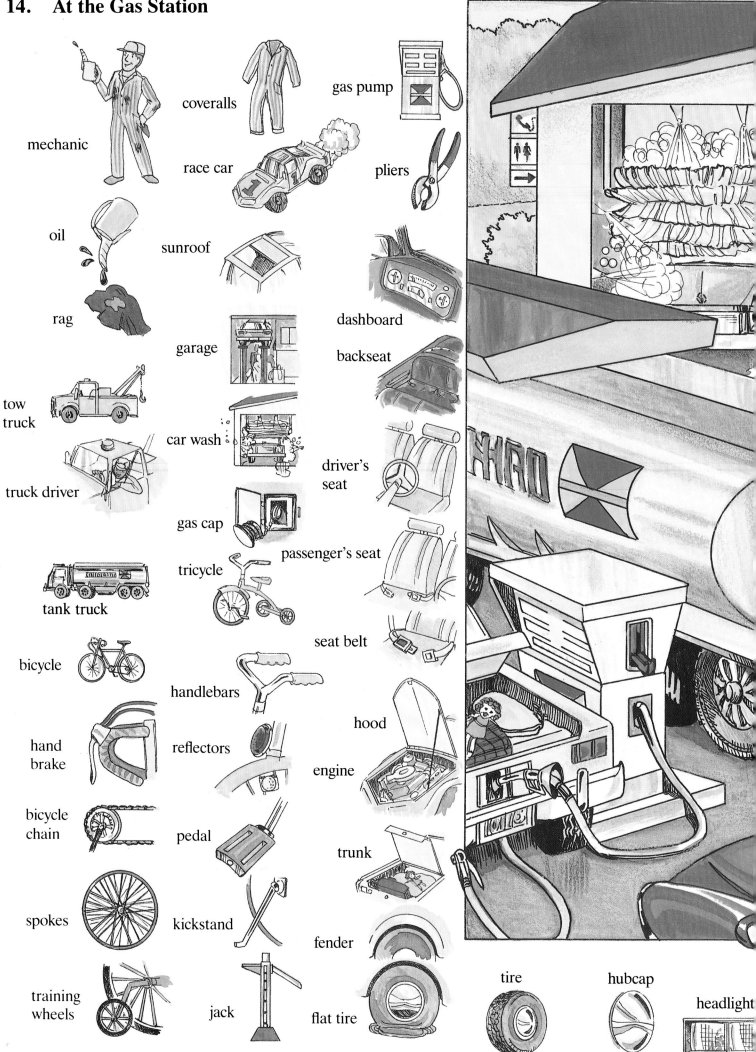

mechanic

coveralls

gas pump

oil

race car

pliers

rag

sunroof

dashboard

garage

backseat

tow truck

car wash

driver's seat

truck driver

gas cap

passenger's seat

tank truck

tricycle

bicycle

seat belt

handlebars

hood

hand brake

reflectors

engine

bicycle chain

pedal

trunk

spokes

kickstand

fender

training wheels

jack

flat tire

tire

hubcap

headlight

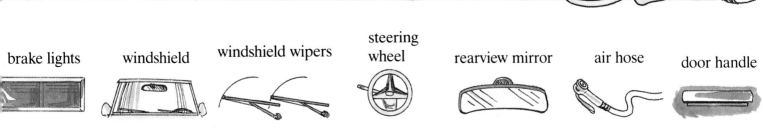

brake lights   windshield   windshield wipers   steering wheel   rearview mirror   air hose   door handle

15. People in Our Community

saleswoman

cook

model

judge

electrician

fire fighter

athlete

doorman

architect

plumber

bus driver

television repairer

taxi driver

fashion designer

tour guide

bookseller

computer programmer

librarian

photographer

gardener

painter

salesman

secretary

weather forecaster

policewoman

veterinarian

disc jockey

reporter

construction worker

florist

tailor

factory worker

optician

butcher

jeweler

foreman

artist

pharmacist

carpenter

banker

sailor

lawyer

cowboy

paramedic

letter carrier

fisherman

astronomer

policeman

16. Going Places (Transportation)

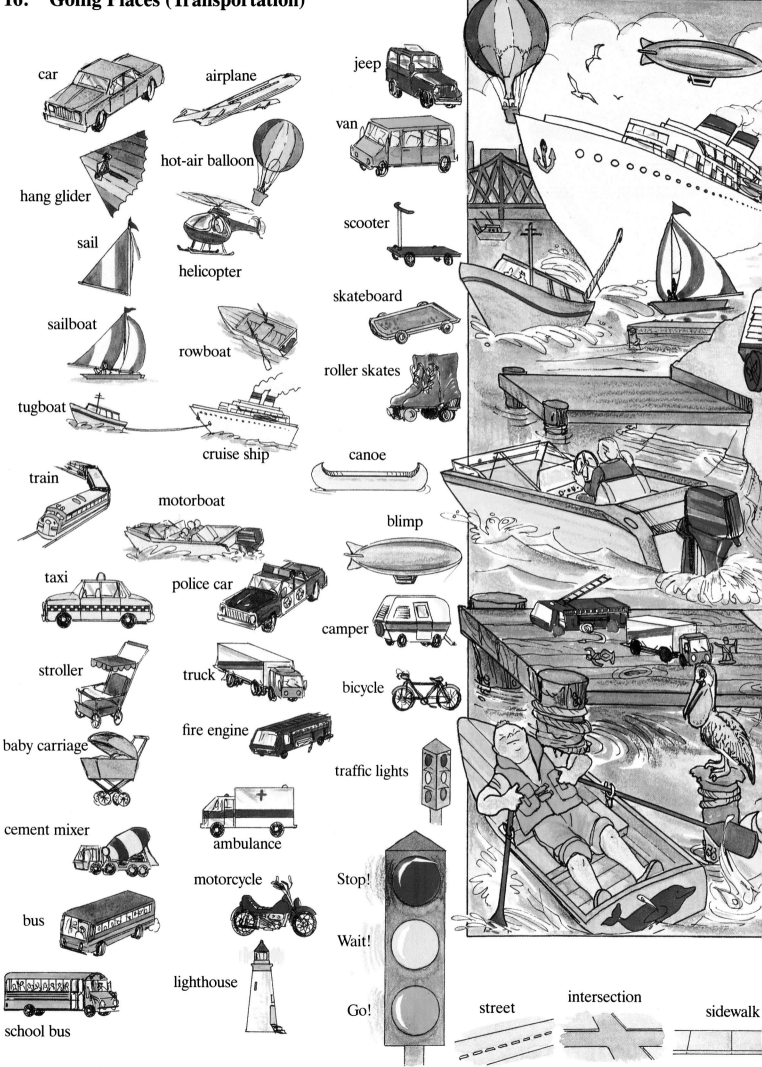

car

airplane

hang glider

hot-air balloon

sail

helicopter

sailboat

rowboat

tugboat

cruise ship

train

motorboat

taxi

police car

stroller

truck

baby carriage

fire engine

cement mixer

ambulance

motorcycle

bus

lighthouse

school bus

jeep

van

scooter

skateboard

roller skates

canoe

blimp

camper

bicycle

traffic lights

Stop!

Wait!

Go!

street

intersection

sidewalk

dock bus stop bridge crosswalk oar boat stop sign

17. The Airport

pilot

air-traffic controller

airplane

copilot

headset

propeller

navigator

control tower

wing

flight attendant

radar screen

engine

baggage handler

flags

landing gear

porter

elevator

runway

baggage claim

metal detector

hangar

baggage check-in

escalator

Concorde

ticket counter

gate

luggage compartment

ticket agent

baggage cart

seat

ticket

customs officer

passenger

snack bar

passport

video camera

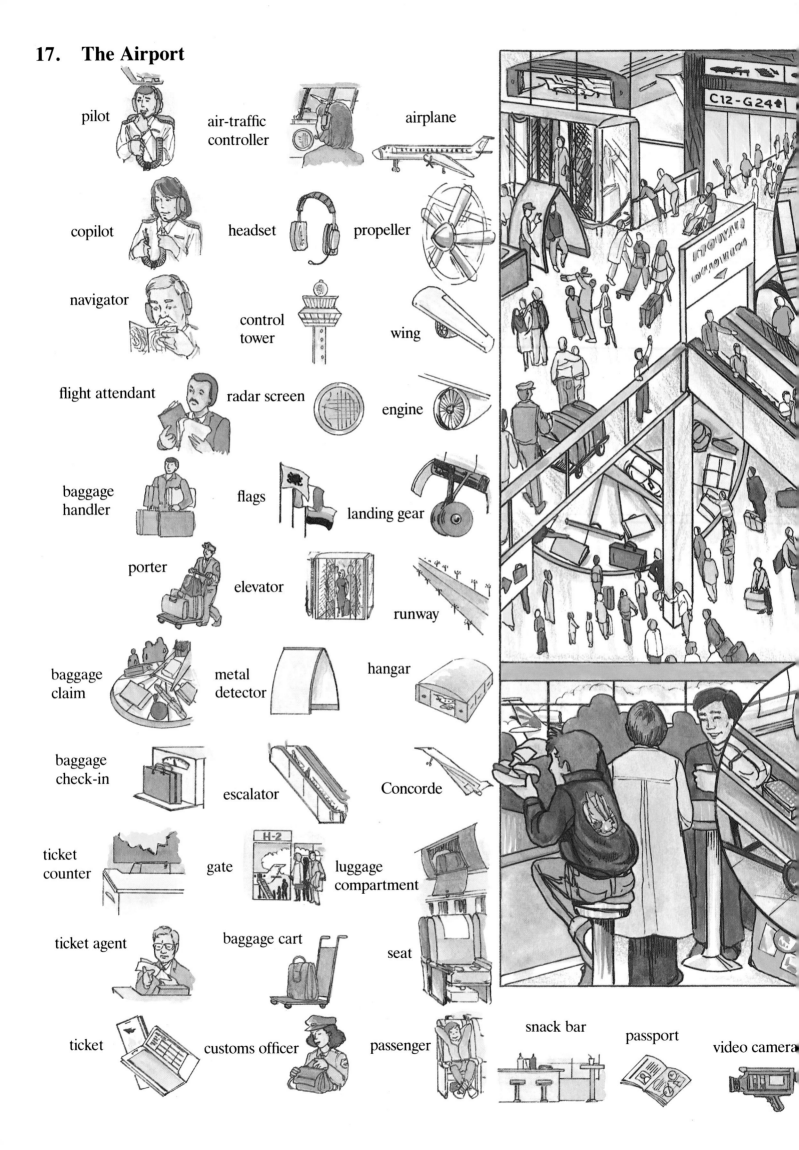

tennis racket   binoculars   camera   purse   suitcase   garment bag   briefcase

18. Sports

gymnastics

goggles

wrestling

cross-country skiing

cycling

soccer

long jump

car racing

baseball

boxing

badminton

net

skates

skating

hurdles

football

golf

medal

horseback riding

baseball

jogging

hockey

tennis

diving

weight lifting

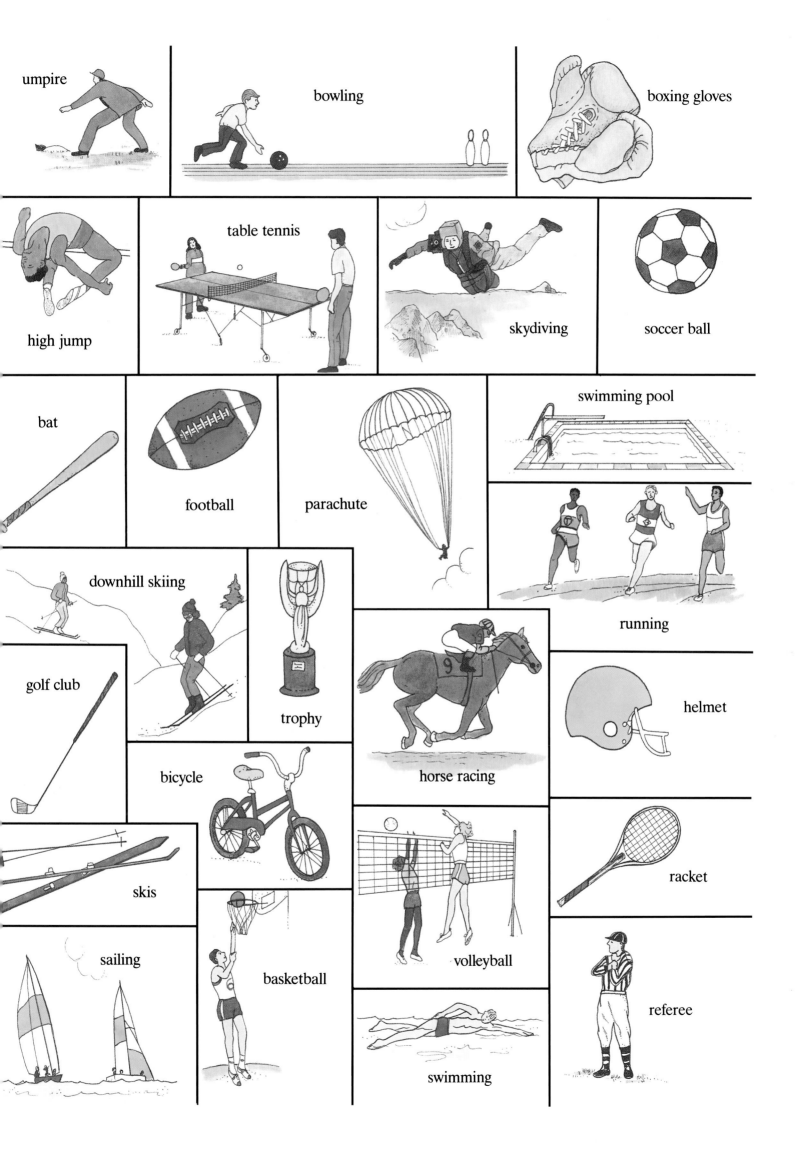

umpire

bowling

boxing gloves

high jump

table tennis

skydiving

soccer ball

bat

football

parachute

swimming pool

running

downhill skiing

trophy

horse racing

helmet

golf club

bicycle

skis

volleyball

racket

sailing

basketball

swimming

referee

19. The Talent Show

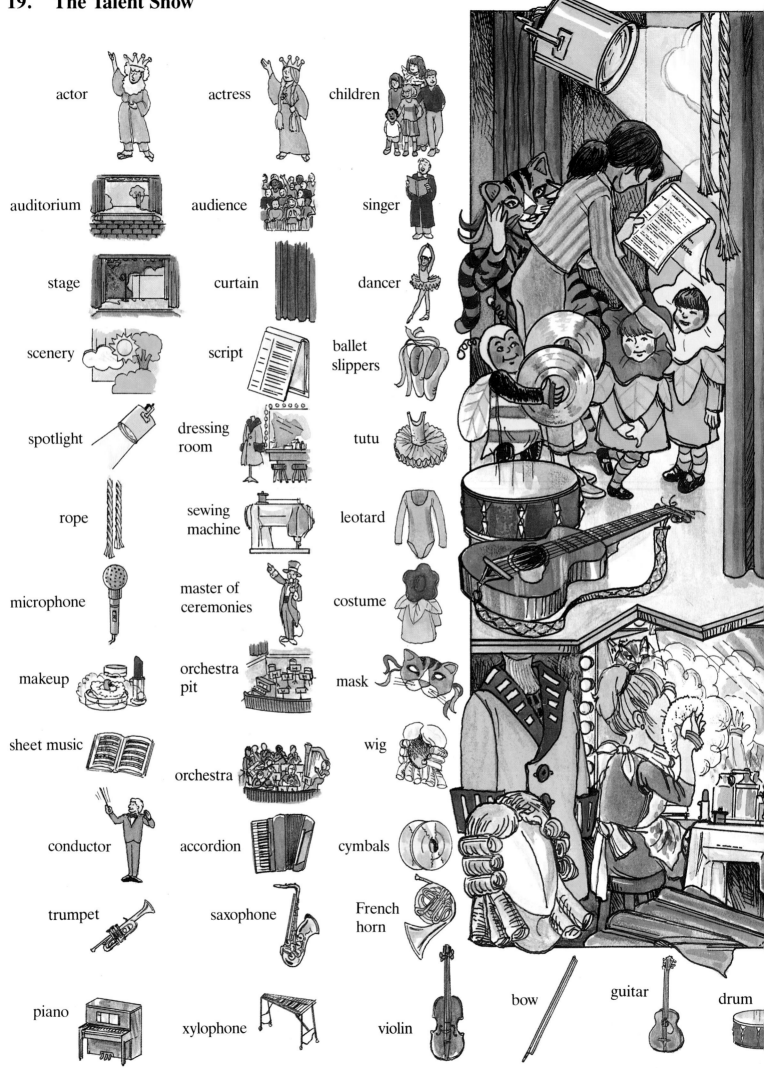

actor

actress

children

auditorium

audience

singer

stage

curtain

dancer

scenery

script

ballet slippers

spotlight

dressing room

tutu

rope

sewing machine

leotard

microphone

master of ceremonies

costume

makeup

orchestra pit

mask

sheet music

wig

orchestra

conductor

accordion

cymbals

trumpet

saxophone

French horn

piano

xylophone

violin

bow

guitar

drum

tuba   flute   trombone   clarinet   cello   strings   harp

20. At the Zoo

zookeeper

rhinoceros

lion

tiger

tiger cub

jaguar

leopard

flamingo

owl

swan

penguin

peacock

eagle

elephant

ostrich

bear

bear cub

polar bear

panda

gorilla

parrot

snake

seal

walrus

hump

camel

animals

fox

wolf

alligator

zebra

giraffe

monkey

hippopotamus

kangaroo

deer

lizard

turtle

horns

wings

feathers

beak

paw   claws   mane   tail   hoof   stripes   spots

21. At the Circus

clown

magician

juggler

ticket booth

popcorn

lion

tickets

stilts

caramel apple

tent pole

baton

big top

balloon

elephant

turban

circus parade

peanuts

flashbulb

lightbulb

film

camera

night

rest rooms

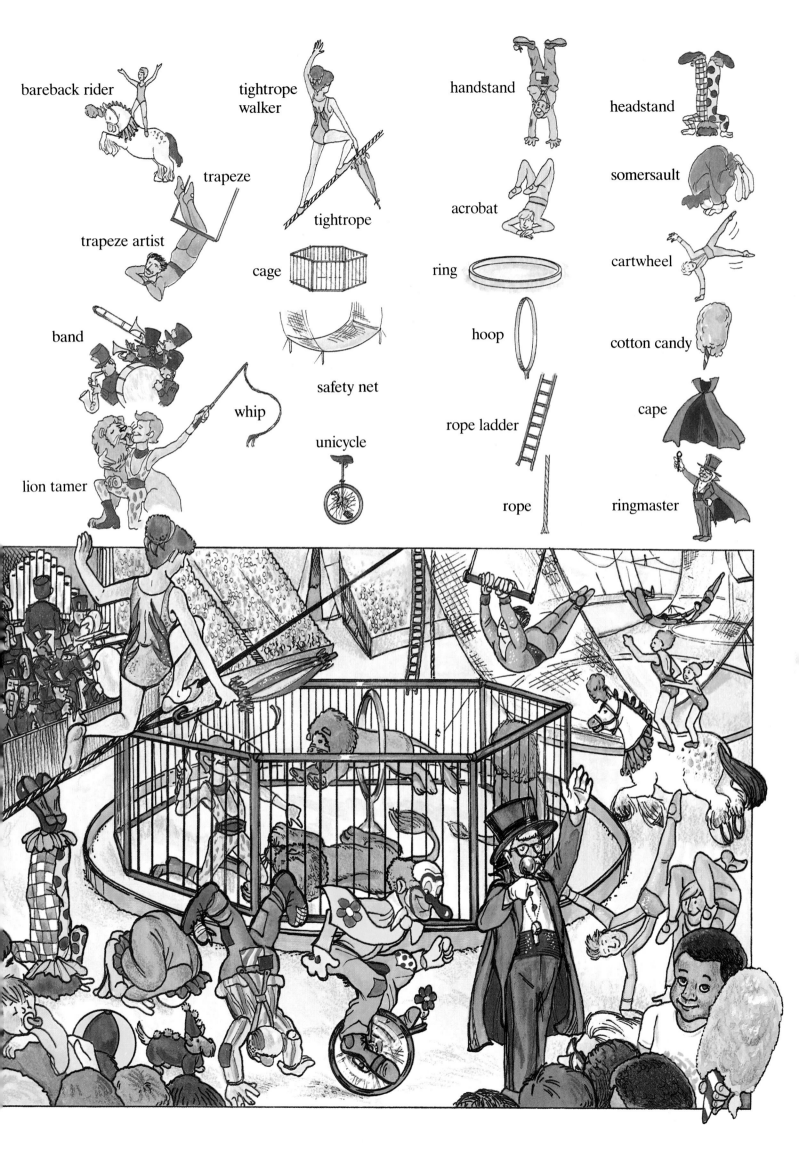

bareback rider

tightrope walker

handstand

headstand

trapeze

somersault

tightrope

acrobat

cartwheel

trapeze artist

cage

ring

band

hoop

cotton candy

safety net

whip

cape

unicycle

rope ladder

lion tamer

rope

ringmaster

22. In the Ocean

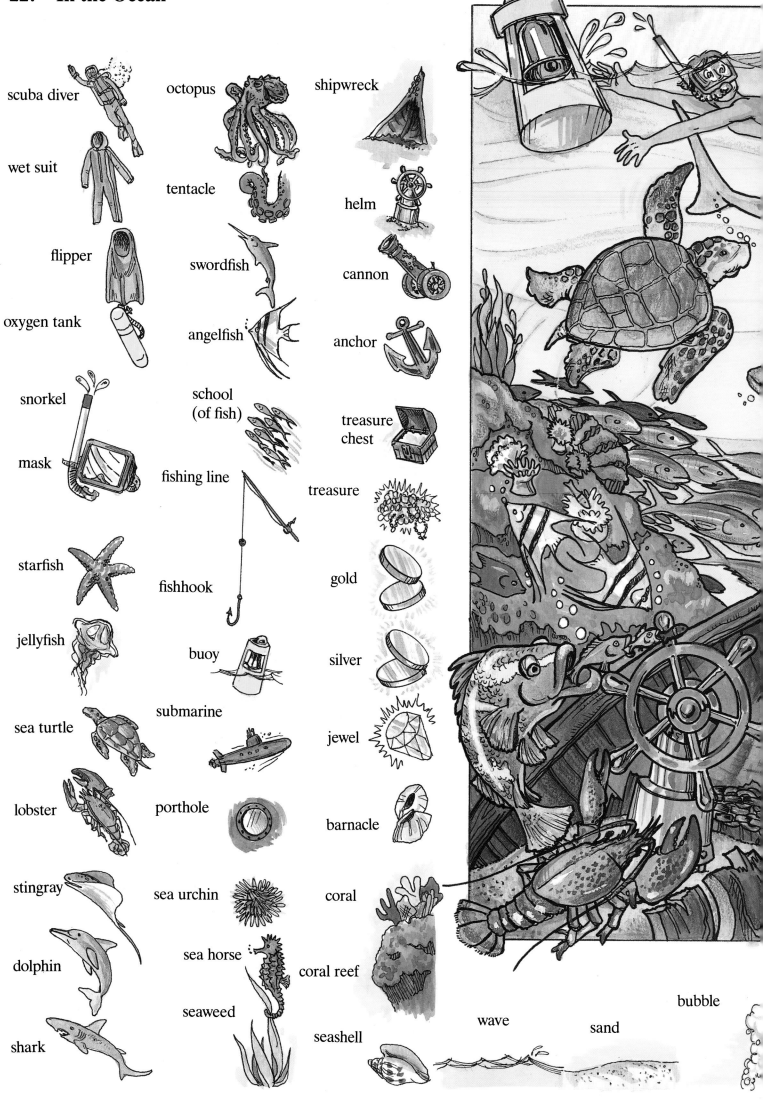

scuba diver

wet suit

flipper

oxygen tank

snorkel

mask

starfish

jellyfish

sea turtle

lobster

stingray

dolphin

shark

octopus

tentacle

swordfish

angelfish

school
(of fish)

fishing line

fishhook

buoy

submarine

porthole

sea urchin

sea horse

seaweed

seashell

shipwreck

helm

cannon

anchor

treasure
chest

treasure

gold

silver

jewel

barnacle

coral

coral reef

wave

sand

bubble

scales
gills
fin
clam
crab
squid
whale

23. Space

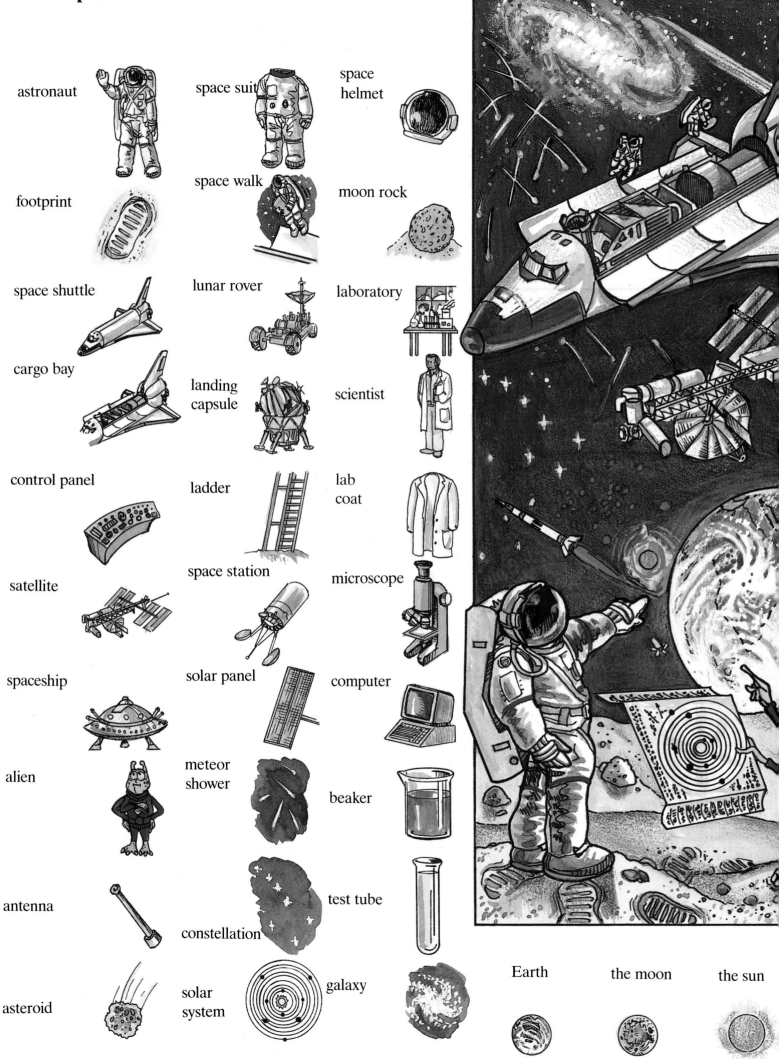

astronaut

space suit

space helmet

footprint

space walk

moon rock

space shuttle

lunar rover

laboratory

cargo bay

landing capsule

scientist

control panel

ladder

lab coat

satellite

space station

microscope

spaceship

solar panel

computer

alien

meteor shower

beaker

antenna

test tube

constellation

asteroid

solar system

galaxy

Earth

the moon

the sun

planet   rings   crater   stars   comet   nebula   rocket   robot

24. Human History

rock

boulder

bone

insect

fern

tree

cave

fur

fire

stick

wheel

flint

arrowhead

club

spear

mammoth

tusk

trunk

bison

paint

cave drawing

hut

corn

wheat

weaver

loom

kiln

potter

pot

clay

cart

basket

leather

fishing

hunter

well

bucket

water

cloth

saber-toothed tiger

crop

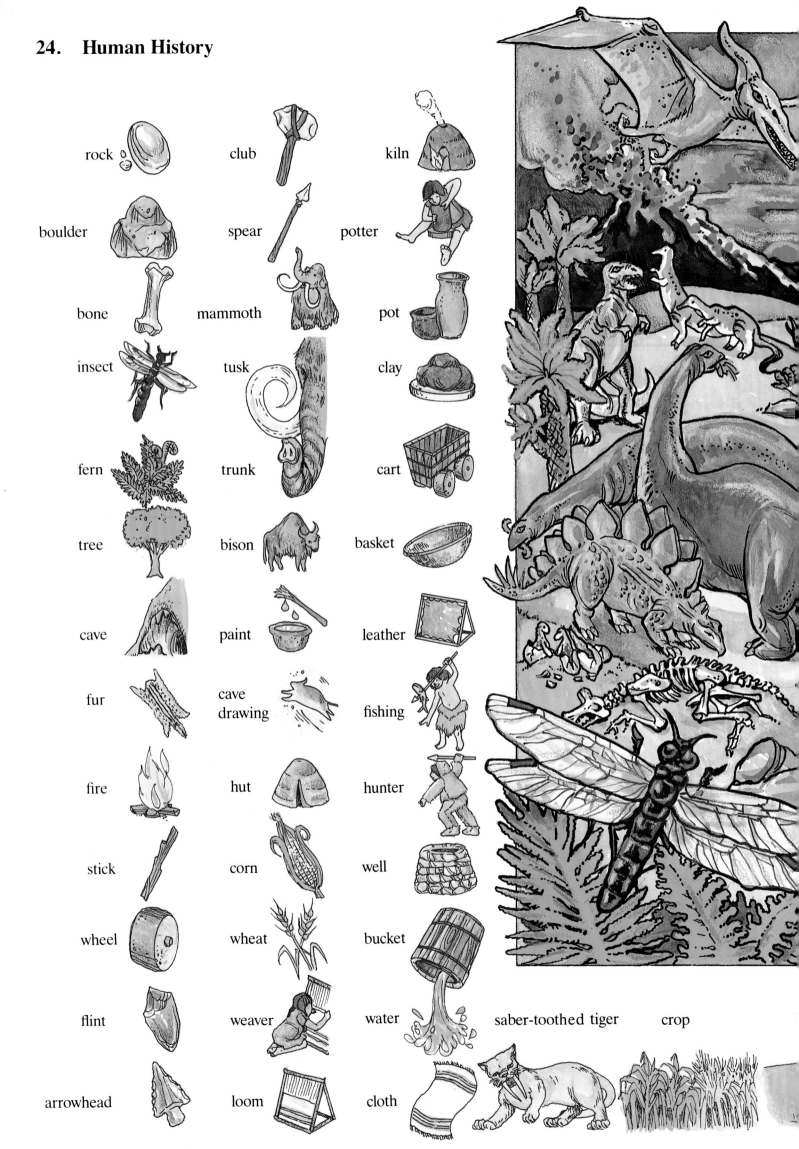

eld   village   cave dwellers   skeleton   dinosaur   pterodactyl

25. The Make-Believe Castle

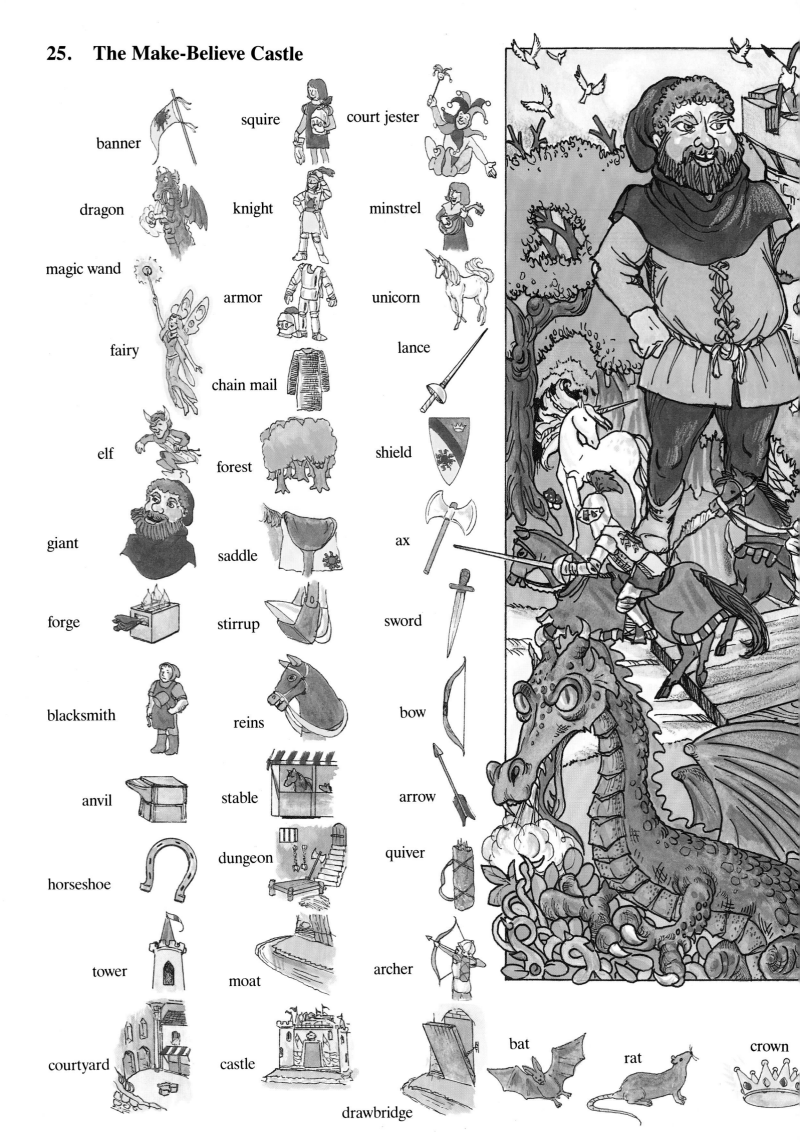

banner

squire

court jester

dragon

knight

minstrel

magic wand

armor

unicorn

fairy

lance

chain mail

elf

forest

shield

giant

saddle

ax

forge

stirrup

sword

blacksmith

reins

bow

anvil

stable

arrow

horseshoe

dungeon

quiver

tower

moat

archer

courtyard

castle

bat

rat

crown

drawbridge

king   queen   princess   prince   throne   spider   spiderweb

26. The Mouse Hunt (Prepositions and Adjectives)

on top of

behind

good

above

in front of

inside

under

outside

bad

next to

soft

tall

wide

narrow

heavy

short

difficult

large

medium

dry

small

wet

fat

full

empty

27. Action Words

to drink   to eat   to sleep   to wash   to skate

to fall   to cry   to laugh   to fly   to write

to read   to play (a game)   to play (an instrument)   to sit down   to stand up

to dance   to walk   to run   to climb   to jump

to drive   to push   to sell   to buy   to ski

to dive   to swim   to paint   to draw   to ride a bicycle

to come

to go

to throw

to catch

to watch

to sing

to talk

to kick

to listen (to)

to think

to roar

to dig

to pour

to juggle

to point (at)

to look for

to find

to give

to receive

to cut

to cook

to open

to close

to take a bath

to teach

to break

to fix

to carry

to pull

to wait

28. Colors

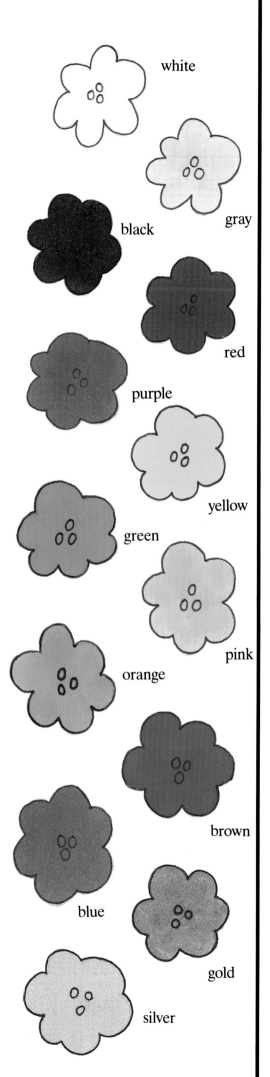

white

gray

black

red

purple

yellow

green

pink

orange

brown

blue

gold

silver

29. The Family Tree

grandmother, grandma

mother, mom

father, dad

son

brother

sister

grandfather, grandpa

uncle

aunt

cousin

cousin

daughter

30. Shapes

square

triangle

circle

rectangle

oval

cube

octagon

sphere

cone

cylinder

31. Numbers

Ordinal Numbers

tenth
ninth
eighth
seventh
sixth
fifth
fourth
third
second
first

Cardinal Numbers

0 zero	½ one-half	1 one	2 two	3 three	4 four	5 five	6 six

16 sixteen	17 seventeen	18 eighteen	19 nineteen	20 twenty	21 twenty-one

28 twenty-eight	29 twenty-nine	30 thirty	31 thirty-one
37 thirty-seven	38 thirty-eight	39 thirty-nine	40 forty
46 forty-six	47 forty-seven	48 forty-eight	49 forty-nine
55 fifty-five	56 fifty-six	57 fifty-seven	58 fifty-eight
64 sixty-four	65 sixty-five	66 sixty-six	67 sixty-seven
73 seventy-three	74 seventy-four	75 seventy-five	76 seventy-six
82 eighty-two	83 eighty-three	84 eighty-four	85 eighty-five
91 ninety-one	92 ninety-two	93 ninety-three	94 ninety-four

100 one hundred	1,000 one thousand	10,000 ten thousand

7	8	9	10	11	12	13	14	15
seven	eight	nine	ten	eleven	twelve	thirteen	fourteen	fifteen

22	23	24	25	26	27
twenty-two	twenty-three	twenty-four	twenty-five	twenty-six	twenty-seven

32	33	34	35	36
thirty-two	thirty-three	thirty-four	thirty-five	thirty-six

41	42	43	44	45
forty-one	forty-two	forty-three	forty-four	forty-five

50	51	52	53	54
fifty	fifty-one	fifty-two	fifty-three	fifty-four

59	60	61	62	63
fifty-nine	sixty	sixty-one	sixty-two	sixty-three

68	69	70	71	72
sixty-eight	sixty-nine	seventy	seventy-one	seventy-two

77	78	79	80	81
seventy-seven	seventy-eight	seventy-nine	eighty	eighty-one

86	87	88	89	90
eighty-six	eighty-seven	eighty-eight	eighty-nine	ninety

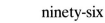 95	96	97	98	99
ninety-five	ninety-six	ninety-seven	ninety-eight	ninety-nine

 00,000

one hundred thousand	one million	one billion

32. A Map of the World

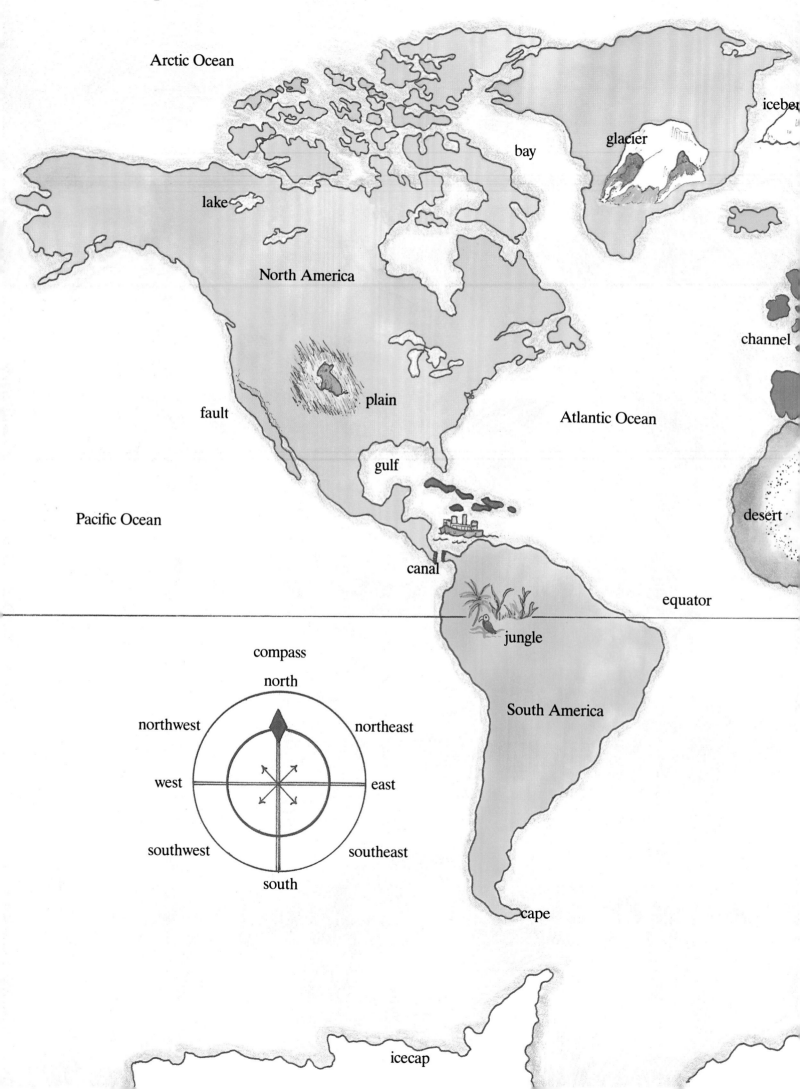

Arctic Ocean

iceber[g]

glacier

bay

lake

North America

plain

fault

Atlantic Ocean

channel

gulf

desert

Pacific Ocean

canal

equator

jungle

compass

north

northwest

northeast

west

east

southwest

southeast

south

South America

cape

icecap

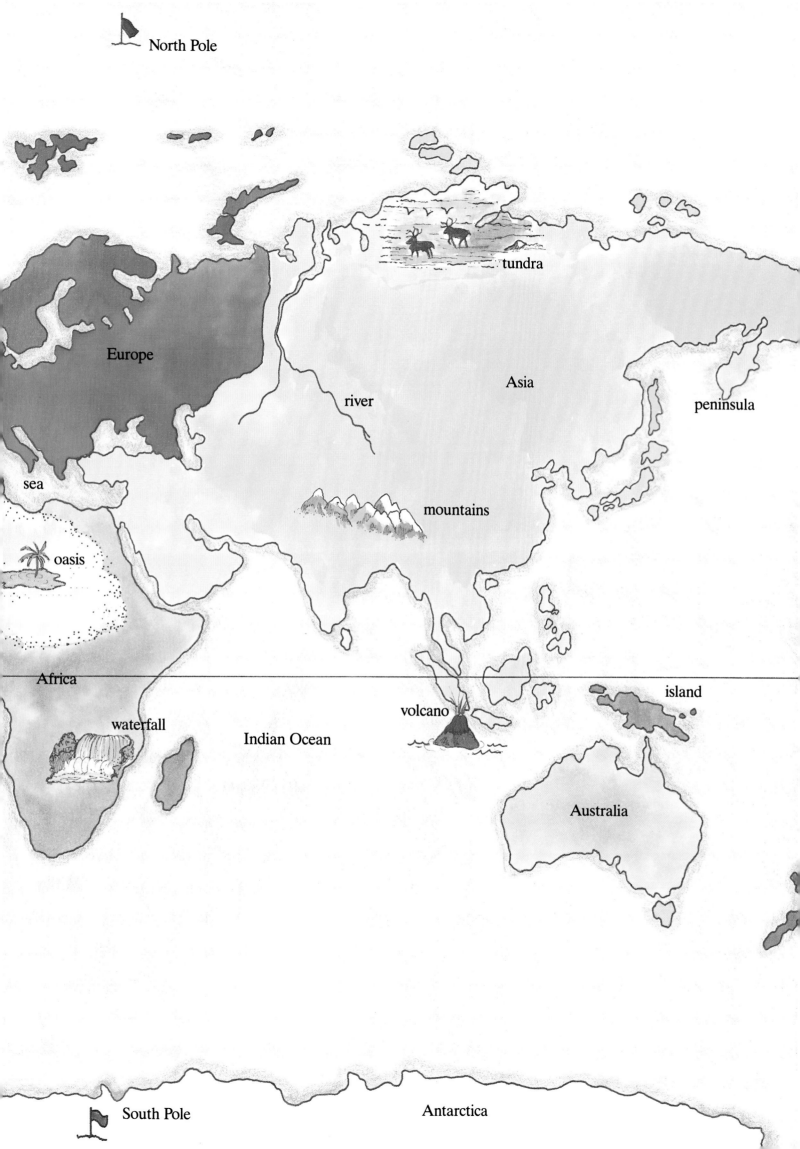

North Pole

Europe

Asia

tundra

river

peninsula

sea

mountains

oasis

Africa

island

volcano

Indian Ocean

waterfall

Australia

South Pole

Antarctica

Index

This index is a list of all words in the dictionary in alphabetical order. After each word, you will find the number of the picture in which you can find the word.